MW00634630

Simply Charming
Table of Contents

Moose on the Porch Quilts
Konda Luckau
665 E 400 S, Payson, UT 84651
801-465-9892
www.moosequilts.com

Commonly Asked Questions about Charm Packs:

1) What is a charm pack?

A charm pack is a package of pre cut 5" squares. Generally a charm pack contains between 30 and 40 squares. All of the fabrics are different because the package includes one square of each fabric in a fabric line excluding panels. Some fabric lines have one charm pack that contains the prints of the line and a separate charm pack that contains the woven fabrics which are commonly plaids of a particular line.

2) Where can I buy charm packs?

Most quilt shops carry charm packs. They are also available online. Right now not all fabric manufacturers make charm packs, but more manufacturers will make them as everyone discovers how much fun they are!

3) What can I do with just one charm pack?

Several patterns in this book can be made with just one charm pack! They include *Charming Fat Quarter* and the baby/table topper size of both *Simply Charming Four Patch* and *Simply Charming Nine Patch*. In addition, every quilt in this book can be made using just one charm pack if you make fewer blocks.

4) What if my charm pack doesn't have enough squares in it?

Because the number of fabrics varies in each charm pack, it is impossible to tell the number of charm packs that each pattern will need. If a charm pack is lacking just a few squares, you have a couple options. First you can always buy another charm pack and use the leftovers to make another quilt like the *Charming Fat Quarter* that doesn't take as many charms. Another thing I have done, is purchase a little extra fabric for the borders or binding and cut a couple 5" squares out of the extra yardage.

5) Can I make these patterns without using charm packs?

Absolutely! Here are some places to find 5" squares:

~ Cut 5" squares out of your *scraps*. All of these quilt patterns make fabulous scrap quilts.

~ Cut 5" squares out of *yardage*. When purchasing yardage for 5" squares, 1/3 yard is a good amount to buy. That will give you two 5" strips with just 2" leftover. These 5" strips can each be cut into 8 squares so 1/3 yard of fabric will give you 16 charm squares.

~ Cut 5" squares out of a *fat quarter*. You can cut twelve 5" squares out of one fat quarter with a couple inches leftover. All the patterns in this book are Fat Quarter Friendly!

6) What if I want to make the pattern larger?

All of the patterns in this book are very simple to enlarge!

One way to make the patterns larger is to make more blocks. Any pattern that is made up of blocks can be enlarged by making more blocks. When making more blocks for a quilt, be aware of whether the number of blocks in a setting is even or odd. For example, *Simply Twisted* is made up of 24 blocks, 4 across and 6 down. To keep the pattern consistent, I would need to stay with even numbers like 6 across and 8 down or 10 across and 10 down. Some quilts like *Simply Charming Four Patch* and *Simply Charming Nine Patch* don't have a pattern formed by the blocks so it doesn't matter if the number of blocks is even or odd. Another thing to consider when you enlarge a quilt by making more blocks is the size of the border. A quilt that started out with a 4" border will need a larger border if it is made into a queen size quilt. The border should be widened or an additional border should be added to keep the quilt in balance.

Another way to make the quilts larger is to add more borders. This method would work nicely on any of the quilts. One thing to think about when adding borders is that it is more pleasing to the eye to have the borders get larger as they go out. For example, *Charming Flowers* has a 2" border and a 5" border. So the next border would need to be 7" or 8". If that is too much border, then you could also change the borders to be 2", 4", and 6" or something else similar. Keep in mind that borders add width and length quickly.

7) Why should I buy a charm pack?
Here are my top ten reasons to buy charm packs:
1) They are just so fun!
2) To quickly achieve a scrappy look.
3) All the fabrics match.
4) You get a piece of an entire fabric line.
5) The squares are already cut.
6) To say, "Thank you!"
7) To say, "Happy Birthday!"
8) To say, "Merry Christmas."
9) They are quicker gifts than making cookies, less fattening, and last longer.
10) To be adventurous!

The reason I picked up my first charm pack was to be adventurous and stretch myself. I rarely buy plaids or grayed fabrics, but I love the comfortable look of quilts made using these fabrics. I decided to challenge myself to make a plaid quilt. I had a terrible time trying to select these fabrics. I fell in love with all the new brown fabrics that had come out, but I still couldn't get to the plaids. I wasn't brave enough to buy fabric I didn't absolutely love.

That was when I purchased a few of *Moda's Chocolat Wovens Charm Packs*. The result was *Simply Twisted*, and I was hooked! I love that quilt, and I never would have made it if I had to buy the fabrics one at a time. My hand would have passed over at least half of them.

Charm Packs are mini-kits. Someone has put together 30-40 fabrics that look fabulous with each other. Occasionally in a charm pack, there are one or two fabrics that I really don't like. I will usually force myself to sew it into the quilt. Many times I find myself surprised that I like the offending fabric just fine once the quilt is finished because of the dimension and depth it adds to the quilt. Other times, I still don't like it, but there are only one or two in the quilt, so I am not disappointed with the overall result. And often I find that the fabric that I thought was so offensive is exactly the fabric that another person loves. That's part of the fun of quilting!

Good luck! I hope you have as much fun with these patterns as I have had making them.
Konda Luckau

e 4: The fabric requirements for the Baby Size should read "36 charm
squares."
e 8: Step 5 should read "five blocks across and six blocks down."
e 13: The block size should read "9 ½" block (9" finished)."
e 15: The cutting instructions step 1b should read "Take 36 of the
m squares and cut them diagonally in half."
e 21: On the squaring up instructions step 1, the small empty
angles should read "7/8."

Simply Charming Four Patch
Block Size: 9 ½" (9" finished)
Quilt Size: 58" x 69"

This pattern is so super simple and yields such fun results that you will want to make this classic pattern over and over again. The full sized pattern is a short twin which is a size that I love! It is perfect to use on the couch watching television or on a chair reading a book. The baby/table topper size only takes 1 charm pack!

Fabric Requirements:
- 80 charm (5") squares
- 1 yard for 2" sashing
- 1 ¼ yards for 6" border
- 3½ yards for backing
- 2/3 yard for binding

Cutting Instructions:
1) From sashing fabric, cut 14-2 ½" strips width of fabric.
   a) Cut 4 of the strips into 15-2 ½" x 9 ½".
   b) Cut 2 of the strips in half.
c) Do not cut the rest of the strips.
2) Cut the border fabric into 6-6 ½" strips width of fabric.

Sewing Instructions:
1) Sew the 80 charm squares into 20 four patch blocks as shown in Figure A. Press.

Figure A

2) After laying out the blocks, sew the vertical sashing pieces onto the right side of the first three four patch blocks in each row as shown in Figure B. Do NOT sew a sashing piece onto the last block.

Figure B

3) Sew each strip together. Press.

4) Refer to Appendix B for instructions on sewing sashing. Sew a horizontal sashing strip to the bottom of the first row as shown in Figure C. Each row is 42½" long so one fabric strip should fit. If it doesn't fit, there is extra from the 4 strips you cut in step 2 to add a little

Figure C

on. Sew and press. Continue sewing a sashing strip to the bottom of the second, third, and fourth rows, NOT the last row.

5) Sew the rows together as in Figure D and press.

6) Take the 4 half sashing strips and sew one of the halves onto each of the remaining four strips.

7) Sew on the first border with these sashing strips by first sewing on the side strips and next sewing on the top and bottom strips.

8) Sew the outer border on in the same manner.

9) Refer to Appendix C method 2 to sew backing.

10) Cut 7—2 ½" strips width of fabric for binding.

Figure D

Baby Size /Table Topper
42" x 42"
9 ½" block (9" finished)

Fabric Requirements:
    30 charm (5") squares
    ¾ yard for 2" sashing
    ½ yard for 3 ½" border
    1 1/3 yards for backing
    ½ yard for binding

Cutting Instructions:
1) From sashing fabric, cut 8-2 ½" strips width of fabric.
    a) Cut 2 of the strips into 6-2 ½" x 9 ½".
    b) Do not cut the rest of the strips.
2) Cut the border fabric into 4-4" strips width of fabric.

Sewing Instructions:
Same sewing instructions as larger size.

Simply Charming Nine Patch
61" x 76 ½"
14" block (13 ½" finished)

This is another classic pattern in a fun, useable size. This baby/table topper size only uses one charm pack! The nine patch unit gives a little more room to play with the colors of the block. You can make them completely scrappy or make a more traditional nine patch block with light and dark colors alternating.

Fabric Requirements:
>   108 charm (5") squares
>   1 ¼ yards for 2" sashing
>   1 1/3 yards for 6" border
>   4 yards for backing
>   2/3 yard for binding

Cutting Instructions:
1) From sashing fabric, cut 14-2 ½" strips width of fabric.
   - a) Cut 3 of the strips into 8-2 ½" x 14".
   - b) Cut 2 of the strips in half.
   - c) Do not cut the rest of the strips.
2) Cut the border fabric into 7-6 ½" strips width of fabric.

Figure A

Sewing Instructions:
1) Sew the 108 charm squares into 12 nine patch blocks. To do this, first sew three sets of three as shown in Figure A. Then sew these sets together matching the corners. Press seams in the directions of the arrows.

2) After laying out the blocks, sew the 14" vertical sashing pieces onto the right of the first two of the nine patch blocks in each row as shown in Figure B. Do NOT sew a sashing piece onto the last block.

Figure B

3) Sew the three squares together to make a strip as shown in Figure C. Press.

4) Refer to Appendix B for instructions on sewing sashing. Take the 4 half sashing strips and sew onto the end of a whole strips. For the fifth horizontal sashing strip, use the one extra 14" strip from step 2 and sew it onto the end of another strip. Now sew one of these horizontal sashing strips to the bottom of the first row as shown in Figure C. Continue sewing a sashing strip to the bottom of the second and third rows. Do NOT sew a sashing strip on the bottom

Figure C

of the last row. There are two 60" sashing strips left for the top and bottom sashing borders.

5) Sew the rows together and press. The quilt should now measure 45" x 60½".

6) Take the remaining four sashing strips and sew two of them together. Sew another pair together so now there are 2 double sashing strips.

7) Sew on the first border using these double sashing strips for the left side and the right side strips. Next sewing on the top and bottom borders using the sashing strips left over from step 4.

8) Sew the outer border on in the same manner.

9) Refer to Appendix C method 2 to cut and sew the backing fabric.

10) Cut 7—2 ½" strips width of fabric for binding.

Figure D

Baby Size / Table Topper
40" x 40"

Fabric Requirements:
    36 charm (5") squares
    ½ yard for 2" sashing
    ½ yard for 3 ½" border
    1 1/3 yards for backing
    ½ yard for binding

Cutting Instructions:
1) From sashing fabric, cut 6-2 ½" strips width of fabric.
    a) Cut 1 of the strips into 2-2 ½" x 14".
    b) Do not cut the rest of the strips.
2) Cut the border fabric into 4-4" strips width of fabric.

Sewing Instructions:
Same sewing instructions as larger size.

Simply Twisted
56½" x 64½"
30 blocks 8 ½" block
(8" finished)

Now for something a little more adventurous. But don't be fooled, this quilt isn't as hard as it looks. As I stated in the introduction, this is the pattern I designed that got me hooked on charm packs. The emphasis in this quilt is in the placement of light and dark fabrics. Because of this emphasis, there are many other possible settings for the blocks. I like how this setting looks like a 16 patch and a pinwheel, a complicated block set on point, or even a 3-Dimensional design!

Fabric Requirements:
      120 charm (5") squares
      ½ yard for 2" border
      1¼ yards for 6" border
      3 yards for backing
      ½ yard for binding

Cutting Instructions:
1) From 2" border fabric, cut 6-2½" strips width of fabric.
2) From 6" border fabric, cut 6-6½" strips width of fabric.

Sewing Instructions:
1) Divide the 120 charm squares into two groups so there are 60 light fabrics and 60 dark fabrics. Take each of those groups and divide them in half. Now there are 2 sets of 30 light squares and 2 sets of 30 dark squares.

Figure A

2) Take 60 charm squares (30 lights and 30 darks) and make 60 half square triangles. Use one light square and one dark square for each triangle as shown in Figure A. See Appendix A for instructions on making half square triangles. Square these triangles up to 4½."

Figure B

3) Take the remaining 60 charm squares (30 lights and 30 darks) and make 48 four patch blocks. Make sure the light and dark fabrics alternate as shown in Figure B. There are two ways to make a four patch block from a charm square:

    a) One way is to cut each charm square into four 2½" squares. Then switch the lights and darks around and sew them back together into four patch blocks. These four patch blocks should measure 4½".

    b) Another way is to sew them similar to the half square triangle—by drawing a line (not diagonal this time) down the middle vertically and placing it right sides together with another square. Then sew ¼" on either side of the line as shown in Figure C. Next cut on the line and press toward the dark fabric. Match this block up with another block sewn the same way. Make sure the darks are on opposite sides and the seams are butted up against each other. Draw a line perpendicular to the seam and sew on either side of that line. Cutting on this line and pressing yields 2 four patch blocks that should measure $4\frac{1}{2}$".

Figure C

4) Now take two of the half square triangles and two of the four patch units and sew together to make one block. Use Figure D to ensure correct placement of the dark and light fabrics. Notice that the triangles are always facing the same direction, but the four patch units are NOT the same.

5) Layout the entire quilt — four blocks across and six blocks down. The quilt requires the same attention to placement as the block does. The blocks are arranged in a pinwheel setting as shown in Figure E. Be sure the lights and darks are always alternating.

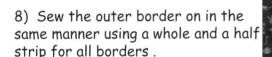

Figure D

6) Sew blocks into their 6 strips and sew strips together as shown in Figure E. Your quilt should now measure $40\frac{1}{2}$" x $48\frac{1}{2}$".

7) Take two of the $2\frac{1}{2}$" border strips and cut them in half. Sew each half onto a whole strip. Sew one of these strips onto the left and right sides of the quilt. Then use the other two of these strips to sew on the top and bottom borders. Refer to Appendix B for instructions on applying borders.

8) Sew the outer border on in the same manner using a whole and a half strip for all borders .

9) Refer to Appendix C method 2 to cut and sew the backing fabric.

10) Cut 6—2 $\frac{1}{2}$" strips width of fabric for binding.

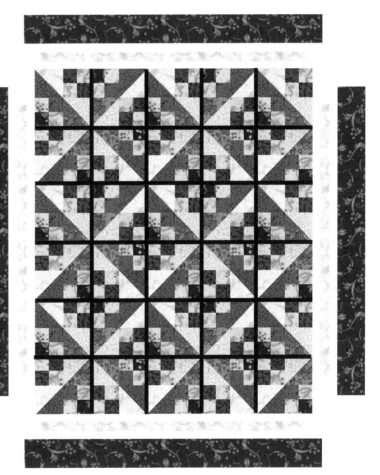

Figure E: Lines are placed on the quilt to more easily see block separation.

Simply Untwisted

54½" x 74½"
24 blocks
8 ½" block (8" finished)

Surprisingly, this quilt is almost the same as Simply Twisted. The block is made up of the same elements. This block is created by keeping the four patch unit in the same direction and rotating the half square triangles. Making those simple changes creates an entirely different quilt!

Fabric Requirements:
     96 charm (5") squares
     2/3 yard for sashing
     1/8 yard for cornerstones
     ½ yard for 2" border
     1 1/3 yards for 6" border
     3½ yards for backing
     ½ yard for binding

Cutting Instructions:
1) From cornerstones fabric cut one 2½" strip width of fabric. Cut the strip into 15—2½" squares.
2) From sashing fabric cut 8—2½" strips width of fabric. Cut these strips into 38—2½" x 8½" rectangles.
3) From 2" border fabric, cut 6-2½" strips width of fabric.
4) From 6" border fabric, cut 7-6½" strips width of fabric. Cut one of the strips in half.

Sewing Instructions:
1) Divide the 96 charm squares into two groups so there are 48 light fabrics and 48 dark fabrics. Take each of those groups and divide them in half. Now there are 2 sets of 24 light squares and 2 sets of 24 dark squares.

2) Take 48 charm squares (24 lights and 24 darks) and make 48 half square triangles. Use one light square and one dark square for each triangle as shown in Figure A. See Appendix A for instructions on making half square triangles. Square these triangles up to 4½."

3) Take the remaining 48 charm squares (24 lights and 24 darks) and make 48 four patch blocks. Make sure the light and dark fabrics alternate as shown in Figure B. There are two ways to make a four patch block from a charm square:

   a) One way is to cut each charm square into four 2½" squares. Then switch the lights and darks around and sew them back together into four patch blocks. These four patch blocks should measure 4½".

Figure A

Figure B

b) Another way is to sew them similar to the half square triangle—by drawing a line (not diagonal this time) down the middle vertically and placing it right sides together with another square. Then sew $\frac{1}{4}$" on either side of the line as shown in Figure C. Next cut on the line and press toward the dark fabric. Match this block up with another block sewn the same way. Make sure the darks are on opposite sides and the seams are butted up against each other. Draw a line perpendicular to the seam and sew on either side of that line. Cutting on this line and pressing yields 2 four patch blocks that should measure $4\frac{1}{2}$".

Figure C

4) Now take two of the half square triangles and two of the four patch units and sew together to make one block. Use Figure D to ensure correct placement of the dark and light fabrics.

5) Layout the entire quilt — four blocks across and six blocks down. The blocks are arranged as shown in Figure E.

Figure D

6) Sew 18 of the vertical sashing strips onto the right of the first three blocks in each row. Do not sew a sashing strip onto the last block. Sew blocks into their 6 strips.

7) Sew the rest of the sashing strips and cornerstones into strips as also shown in Figure E. Press seams toward the sashing strips.

6) Sew strips together as shown in Figure E. Your quilt should now measure $38\frac{1}{2}$" x $58\frac{1}{2}$".

7) Take two of the $2\frac{1}{2}$" border strips and sew them together to make one long border strip. Repeat with another pair of strips. Sew one of these double strips onto the left side and another onto the right side of the quilt. Using the 2 remaining border strips, sew on the top and bottom borders. Refer to Appendix B for instructions on applying borders.

8) Sew the outer border on in the same manner using a double strip for the side borders and a whole and a half strip for the top and bottom borders.

9) Refer to Appendix C method 2 to cut and sew the backing fabric.

9) Cut 7—2 $\frac{1}{2}$" strips width of fabric for binding.

Figure E

Simply Twisted

Charming Birds

Charming Flowers

Charming Flowers

52½" x 70½"
24 blocks
9" block (9½" finished)

After a colder than usual winter, I was ready for spring. I was given 4 fat quarters that made me feel hopeful that spring would come. After finding coordinating fabrics in my stash and at the quilt shop, this quilt came about. This was one quilt that I cut my own charm squares out of fat quarters so the flowers looked the same. It would also look fun with each flower being made out of different fabrics of the same color.

Fabric Requirements:

96 charm (5") squares
1¼ yards for background
1/3 yard for flower centers
½ yard for 2" border
1¼ yards for 6" border
3¼ yards for backing
2/3 yard for binding

Cutting Instructions:

1) Refer to Commonly Asked Questions number 5 on page 4 for information on cutting charm squares out of fat quarters if you choose.
2) From background fabric, cut 14—2¾" strips width of fabric. Cut strips into 192—2¾" squares.
3) From flower center fabric, cut 5—2" strips width of fabric. Cut strips into 96—2" squares.
4) Cut the inner border fabric into 5—2½" strips width of fabric.
5) Cut the outer border fabric into 6—6½" strips width of fabric.

Sewing Instructions:

1) This quilt is made up of 96 identical petal units. It takes three steps to turn a charm square into a flower petal.

2) First, draw a diagonal line with a pencil on the back of all of the small background squares and the flower centers.

3) Take one of the small background squares. Place it on one corner of a charm square with right sides of the fabric together as shown in Figure A. Sew on the line. Trim seam allowance to ¼".

Figure A

4) Press open as shown in Figure B. Sew all 96 charm squares in this manner.

Figure B   Figure C

5) Take another small background square. Place it on an adjacent corner of a charm square with right sides together. Repeat the same process as in step 3 resulting in the flower petal shown in Figure C.

6) Make the flower center using the same process.   Flower centers must be sewn onto the same corner of each charm square. As shown in Figure D, the flower center is sewn onto the bottom left corner.

Figure D

7) Once the petal units are complete, the flowers can be sewn together by rotating the petals around the center as shown in Figure E.

8) Layout the quilt 4 flowers across and 6 flowers down. Sew flowers into rows then sew rows together. The quilt should now measure $36\frac{1}{2}$" x $54\frac{1}{2}$".

9) Cut one of the inner border strips in half. Sew each half onto a whole strip. Sew one of these long strips onto the left side and another onto the right side.   Refer to Appendix B for instructions on applying borders. Sew a border strip onto the top and bottom in the same manner.

Figure E

10) Cut two of the outer border strips in half and sew each half onto a whole strip. Apply outer borders in the same manner as inner borders.

11) Refer to Appendix C method 2 to cut and sew the backing.

12) Cut 7—2 $\frac{1}{2}$" strips width of fabric for binding.

Charming Birds

64½" x 88½"
24 blocks
12 ½" block (12" finished)

Charm squares are the perfect size to make this quilt. I was surprised at the ease with which this quilt went together. By using half square triangles and squaring up along the way, these birds practically "flew" into place. The only thing to watch was sewing the main diagonal seam. With a little precaution, even the bias seam doesn't slow this quilt down.

Fabric Requirements:

    72 charm (5") squares
    2¼ yard for background
    ¾ yard for 2" border
    1½ yards for 6" border
    5 yards for backing
    2/3 yard for binding

Cutting Instructions:

1) Cut background fabric into 5—5" strips width of fabric.
    a) Cut into 36—5" squares.
    b) Take 36 of these small background squares
and cut them diagonally in half.
2) Also cut background fabric into 4—12 7/8" strips width of fabric.
    a) Cut these strips into 12—12 7/8" squares
    b) Cut each square diagonally resulting in 24
triangles.
3) From 2" border fabric, cut 7-2½" strips width of fabric.
4) From 6" border fabric, cut 8-6½" strips width of fabric.

Sewing Instructions:

1) Take 36 charm squares and 36-5" background squares and make half square triangles. Square up to 4½". Refer to Appendix A for instructions on making half square triangles.

2) Now to sew the birds. Layout 3 half square triangle units and three half charm squares as shown in Figure A. Sew each row together being careful to match the points indicated with a circle. Press seams in the direction of the arrows.

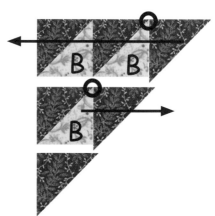

Figure A: B refers to the background fabric.

3) Sew rows together as shown in Figure B. Be careful to match the points indicated with a circle. Press seams in the directions of the arrow. Take care when pressing not to distort the block.

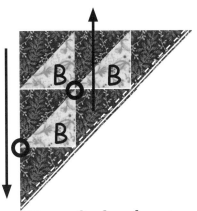

4) Next trim the ¼" seam allowance as shown in Figure B. The dotted line represents the sewing line which goes right through the two corner seams. The solid line represents the cutting line which is ¼" away from the intersections. Line up the ¼" mark on ruler with the two intersections along the long diagonal side of the block and trim.

Figure B: B refers to the background fabric.

5) Repeat using all half square triangle units and charm triangles. One block takes 3 half square triangle units and 4 charm triangles. When finished, there will be 24 bird units.

6) To finish off the block, sew the bird unit to a background square as shown in Figure C. This last seam is a long bias seam that likes to stretch. To prevent stretching, place 3-5 pins along the seam. Also, after placing right sides together, stitch with the bird unit on top. This allows care to be taken with the two intersections while sewing.

Figure C

7) Layout quilt as shown in Figure D. This is a rotated setting. There are many other settings to experiment with at this point.

8) After deciding on a layout, sew the blocks in rows of 4. Then sew the rows together as shown in Figure D. Your quilt should now measure 48½" x 72½".

9) Take two of the 2½" border strips and sew them together. Repeat with two more 2½" border strips. Sew one of these strips onto the left and right sides of the quilt.

10) Take one of the 2½" border strips and cut it in half. Sew each half onto a whole strip. Use these two steps to sew on the top and bottom borders. Refer to Appendix B for instructions on applying borders.

11) Sew the outer border on in the same manner using a double strip for all borders .

12) Refer to Appendix C method 3 to cut and sew the backing fabric.

13) Cut 8—2 ½" strips width of fabric for binding.

Figure D

Charming Fat Quarter
37" x 37"

Take a fat quarter, a charm pack, and a little yardage, and this is the result. A friend of mine gave me the idea for this quilt. After she explained it to me, I went home and made two of them! It is a super fast baby quilt or table topper and a fun quilt to buy fabric for.

Fabric Requirements:
    24 charm (5") squares
    1 fat quarter (center)
    2/3 yard borders (6-3" strips)
    1/3 yard binding
    1¼ yards backing

Cutting Instructions:
1) Cut fat quarter into 18" square
2) Cut border fabric into 6-3" strips width of fabric.
    a) Cut two strips each into 1-3"x18" and 1-3"x23" so there are two of each size.
    b) Cut two strips into 2-3"x32" strips.
    c) Cut two strips into 2-3"x37" strips.

Sewing Instructions:
1) Sew the 18" border strips to the sides of the center square. Sew the 23" border strips to the top and bottom of the center square.

2) Layout the quilt as shown in Figure A.

3) Next sew the 5 left squares into a strip and the 5 right squares into another strip. Also sew the 7 top squares into one strip and the 7 bottom squares into another strip.

4) Sew the left strip of squares onto the center and the right strip of squares onto the center. Then sew the top and bottom strips of squares onto the center.

Figure A

5) Sew the 32" strips onto the left and right sides and the 37" strips onto the top and bottom.

6) Cut 6—2½" strips width of fabric for binding.

Larger Size
49" x 49"

This quilt is perfect to enlarge by adding an extra border.

Fabric Requirements:
    24 charm (5") squares
    1 fat quarter (center)
    2/3 yard for 2½" borders
    1 yard for 6½" borders
    ½ yard binding
    2¼ yards backing

Cutting Instructions:
1) Cut fat quarter into 18" square
2) Cut 2½" border fabric into 6-3" strips width of fabric.
    a) Cut two strips each into 1-3"x18" and 1-3"x23" so there are two of each size.
    b) Cut two strips into 2-3"x32" strips.
    c) Cut two strips into 2-3"x37" strips.
3) Cut 6½" border fabric into 5-6½" strips width of fabric.
    a) Cut one of the strips in half.

Sewing Instructions:
1) Follow steps 1-5 of the regular size pattern.

2) Take two of the 6½" border strips sew them onto the left side and right side of the quilt.

3) Take the two half 6½" border strips and sew them each onto a whole strip. Sew these two long strips onto the top and bottom of the quilt.

4) Refer to Appendix C method 1 to cut and sew the backing fabric.

5) Cut 5-2½" strips width of fabric for binding.

Charming Queen
86" x 90½"

As I showed some quilters *Charming Fat Quarter*, I was asked how to make the quilt bigger. *Charming Queen* is the result. The center is perfect for a large scale fabric or a panel print.

Fabric Requirements:
>   100 charm (5") squares
>   1 yard for center
>   3½ yard for borders
>   6¼ yards for backing
>   2/3 yard for binding

Cutting Instructions:
1) Cut center fabric into a rectangle 36" x 40½".
2) Cut border fabric into the following:
>   a) 4—3" strips width of fabric,
>   b) 6—5" strips width of fabric, and
>   c) 8—9½" strips width of fabric.

Sewing Instructions:
1) Take the 4-3" border strips. Sew one to the left side and another to the right side of the center square. Press. Next sew the 3" border strips to the top and bottom of the center square. Press. Refer to Appendix B for instructions on sewing borders.

2) Layout the quilt as shown on the opposite page.

3) Sew the charm squares into strips of 10, 11, 14, or 15 squares as shown in the assembly diagram layout on the opposite page.

4) Next sew the strips of squares to the quilt. Begin by sewing the border strips of 10 squares to the left side and right side. Then sew the border strips of 11 squares to the top and bottom.

5) Continue sewing the borders on as shown in the assembly diagram on the opposite page.

6) Refer to Appendix C method 3 for cutting and sewing the backing.

7) Cut 8—2½" strips for binding.

Assembly Diagram

Appendix A: Half Square Triangles

This is one method for making half-square triangles. This method uses two squares of the same size and results in two half square triangles. A $\frac{1}{4}$" presser foot is required for this method unless there is a $\frac{1}{4}$" mark on the front of a different presser foot. Guides on the sewing machine do not work with this method. The other tool required is a square ruler the size that the unit is being squared up to. With all the quilts in this book, that would be a $4\frac{1}{2}$" square ruler. A slightly larger square ruler will also work, but is not quite as quick.

Sewing Instructions:

1) Take two different colored squares of the same size. All the quilts in this book start with 5" charm squares.

Figure A

2) On the back of one square, draw a diagonal line with a pencil that connects two opposite corners of the square as shown by the solid line in Figure A.

3) Pin this square to the second square so right sides of the fabric are together and the pencil line is showing.

4) Sew a $\frac{1}{4}$" seam on either side of the line as shown by the dotted lines in Figure A. With a $\frac{1}{4}$" presser foot, the pencil line will line up on the edge of the presser foot.

5) Cut along the pencil line with a rotary cutter or scissors. Press. Generally seams are pressed towards the dark triangle as shown in Figure B. To press half square triangle units, first press shut with the dark triangle on top. Next lift the dark fabric up and finger press open. Press gently taking care to lift and press with the iron rather than "ironing" the fabric. Ironing will distort the fabric while pressing will not.

Figure B

6) Repeat with the other triangle. Now there are two half square triangle units that need to be squared up.

Squaring Up Instructions:

1) All of the half square triangles in this book will be "squared up" to $4\frac{1}{2}$". Often after sewing half square triangles, these units will be a little skewed. Starting with a 5" charm square gives an ☐" to trim the unit into a $4\frac{1}{2}$" square. Generally that ☐" is just the right amount of extra fabric for squaring up.

2) Before squaring up, the half square triangle unit must be pressed as explained in step 6 above. Then place one half square triangle unit on a cutting mat right side up. Take a $4\frac{1}{2}$" square ruler and place it on top of the unit. Match the ruler to the unit in two places. First match opposite corners of the ruler to the diagonal seam of the half square triangle. Second look around the edges of the ruler and make sure the unit either lines up with the ruler or sticks out a little from underneath.

3) Hold ruler firmly. With a rotary cutter trim the right and top sides along the ruler. Carefully turn the unit and the ruler to trim the other two sides.

4) Now the half square triangle unit is a perfect $4\frac{1}{2}$" square as shown in Figure C that will sew nicely into any pattern!

Figure C

Appendix B: Midge's Perfect Borders and Sashing

Care must be taken when sewing on long pieces of fabric. This method of applying sashing and borders is perfect for the beginning (and experienced) quilter. Using this method will ensure sashing and border lay flat. They will not be too tight leaving a "pregnant" quilt, and they will not be too loose leaving borders that ripple and wave. What it does not do is ensure that a quilt is square. This method maintains the shape of the interior of the quilt. So if your blocks and rows are square and pressed neatly, this method will preserve those square angles and your entire quilt will remain square. The sewing instructions will be given for applying borders. This method also works for sewing on long sashing strips.

Preparation:
1) Press everything neatly. Press blocks that sashing will be applied to and press the entire quilt that borders will be applied to.

2) Make sure the sashing or border strips are a little longer than the blocks or quilt they are being applied to and that they are also free of creases.

3) The only tools you need are pins. Have plenty on hand.

Sewing Instructions:
1) Stand up. First we will pin the left border. Line up the top left corner of the quilt and the end of the first border strip right sides together. Pin.

2) Hold the pinned area and gently shake the quilt and the border. This allows gravity to help line up the quilt and border for a few more inches. Pin. Take care not to stretch either the quilt or the border. Continue down the border by holding the next pin, shaking out, lining up the quilt and border, and placing the next pin. Pin approximately every 8".

3) After the border is pinned, trim the border even with the end of the quilt. Take care to make this cut straight and square to prevent "dog-eared" corners.

4) Sew on border with a $\frac{1}{4}$" seam allowance. Take care not to stretch either the quilt or the border. Holding onto the pins while sewing will prevent uneven stretching. Press.

5) Repeat with the right border and then with the top and bottom borders. Generally borders are applied in this order:
> 1) left and right inside borders
> 2) top and bottom inside borders
> 3) left and right outside borders
> 4) top and bottom outside borders

If there are more borders, they are added in the same order with left and right borders generally added before top and bottom borders.

6) Viola! A few pins and standing up to let gravity help makes quick work out of long unruly borders and sashing strips.

Appendix C: Piecing a Back

Many quilt shops carry backing fabric that is 90" wide or 108" wide which is handy because it eliminates the need to piece a back for the quilt. This fabric is usually very reasonably priced. However, for many reasons, quilters often need to seam fabric together to make a back large enough for the back of a quilt.

First, when figuring out how to seam a back, be sure the back is several inches larger both in the length and the width than the quilt top. If the quilt is 40" (sometimes 42") wide or smaller, then one length of fabric will be enough. The following examples apply when the width is greater than 40". Then we need to take the length into consideration when deciding how to piece the back together.

1) Length of the quilt is between 40" and 60"
- Take the width of the fabric and round up to a nice number. That is the whole length. To find the rest of the fabric needed, take half of that amount and add it to the whole length. That is how much fabric needs to be purchased.
- Cut the fabric into 2 pieces--one piece will be the "whole" length and the second piece will be the "half" length. Take the "half" length and cut it in half lengthwise. Lengthwise is the long side that is parallel to the selvedge. This cut will often be made on or close to the fold put in the fabric by the manufacturer.
- Sew the two short sides of this "half" length together so that now it is as long as the "whole" length. Sew onto the two lengths together as shown in Figure A.

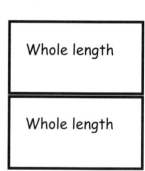
Figure A

2) Length of the quilt is between 60" and 80"
- Most of the quilts in this book require this type of seaming. It is also the quickest.
- Take the width of the fabric and round up to a nice number. That is the whole length.
- Two lengths are need so the amount is doubled. That is how much fabric needs to be purchased.
- Cut the fabric in half so there are two "whole" lengths.
- Sew the two lengths together along the selvedge as shown in Figure B.

Figure B

3) Length of the quilt is between 80" and 100"
- Take the width of the fabric and round up to a nice number. That is the whole length. To find the rest of the fabric needed, take half of that amount and add it to TWO whole lengths. That is how much fabric needs to be purchased.
- Cut the fabric into two "whole" lengths and one "half" length.
- Take the "half" length and cut it in half lengthwise. Lengthwise is the long side that is parallel to the selvedge. This cut will often be made on or close to the fold put in the fabric by the manufacturer.
- Sew the two short sides of this "half" length together so that now it is as long as the "whole" length. Sew onto the three lengths together as shown in Figure C.

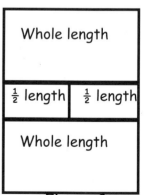
Figure C